Corey Van Landingham

LOVE

LETTER

TO

WHO

OWNS

THE

HEAVENS

Love Letter to Who Owns the Heavens.
Copyright © 2022 Corey Van Landingham.

Library of Congress Cataloging-in-Publication Data

IDENTIFIERS: LCCN 2021015288
ISBN 978-1-946482-61-7 (paperback)
subjects: LCGFT: Poetry.
Classification:
LCC PS3622.A585494 L68 2022 | DDC 811/.6--DC23
LC record available at https://lccn.loc.gov/2021015288

Cover art: Winged Victory of Samothrace,
Musée du Louvre, MA 2369

Designed and composed
in Adobe Caslon by Dede Cummings.

First paperback edition January 2022

Tupelo Press
P.O. BOX 1767
NORTH ADAMS, MASSACHUSETTS 01247
(413) 664-9611 / FAX: (413) 664-9711
editor@tupelopress.org / www.tupelopress.org

Tupelo Press is an award-winning independent literary press that publishes fine
fiction, nonfiction, and poetry in books that are a joy to hold as well as read.
Tupelo Press is a registered 501(c)(3) nonprofit organization, and we rely on public
support to carry out our mission of publishing extraordinary work that may be
outside the realm of the large commercial publishers. Financial donations are
welcome and are tax deductible.

Contents

for C

The air is filled with strangely human birds. Machines, the daughters of man and having no mother, live a life from which passion and feeling are absent—and would that be nothing new?

—APOLLINAIRE

Far from you I measure the nothingness of flesh.

—SARTRE *to* DE BEAUVOIR

Desiderata

We met among ruins. I was so much the dog, in Athens, on the grass
panting for you. In Segovia you pushed my cheek against the aqueduct
until it bled. Darling, we are such sweet modern machines
when our parts are working. Someday we won't fall so apart, or need
our blood. I'll project us onto a screen and feel exactly nostalgic.
My scent will be textable, too-much. The damage I could do
with just a button. When the planets collide in their pinball trajectories,
when the panic of geese breaks up the sky like a brick through
the window, how can I not think we're doomed? If there is a future
and I exist in it, if I built a dwelling with my own devices,
moved there alone, what then of the body? Would, at night,
it call out fevered to be the mule to some man's lead? Would it be
yours? Or an historical site you'll visit, with another body to press
against it, like all our atoms will someday be pressing against
each other. What hope. Love, give us all at once an ending
to look forward to. I want that—quick eternal, the bathtub full
of water, which, like us, is nothing without oxygen. I am nothing
much, it's true. I own four acres of star-thistled land in California.
It's the perfect place to wait out an earthquake. No street names,
the water potable. There is no one else for miles around.
They say Rome wasn't built in a day, but wasn't one day it fallen?

In The Year of No Sleep

physics loosened. Material things
                blurred. In class I saw
the metal chair's particles
           move. It was all so
Newtonian. I taught the mechanics
                of meter to students nodding
off and at night the Old Poets'
          syllables stair-stepped
around my room. Why should the apple,
             asked Newton, always
descend perpendicularly to the ground?
       Why should the chalk fall
to the linoleum, the stack of papers
             fly across the floor?
Inelegant movements of the sleepless.
         Long nights I would make my phone
bright and watch the simulated
             stock ticker make senseless
money for people I will never
          see. Across the country men
make invisible machines
             in a room, I imagine, dark
and whirring with the noises
         their monitors emit. In Minot,
North Dakota, for instance, drone
            operations target men

we will no longer, signed papers say,
            torture. We will not keep them
from sleep or force-feed them
                rectally. We will not
touch them. Once we mastered
        gravity wasn't distance
a thing of the past. That the earth draws
                it down, the fruit, the flight,
as matter, Newton found, draws the earth
        back to it. In California
nights are clear and frenzied.
                And in the morning my students
explained why they dislike
        the spondee. For its excessive force.

Love Letter to Nike Alighting on a Warship

I could not know how like the drone you would become,
standing below your grandeur at the Louvre.

Ears stripped, mouthless—Good Girl! Broken Goddess!
You were already, were still, the woman commemorating

a long war. All breast to mark man's arête, Hellenistic
in a fierce headwind, drama and theatre. You, sentinel,

see all. Here, wrote Rilke, there is no place that does not
see you. Apollo, god of truth and light, omniscient

without a head. Poetry and war, senseless. "The world"—
Dickinson in a letter—"is sleeping in ignorance

and error." At night, now, the unmanned machines
still have to, somewhere, touch down. Grounded,

men clean the wings with their own hands. Stand back, a docent
warned me then. You're getting, he said, too close to her.

The Goodly Creatures of Shady Cove

Above the boat launch, four boys test themselves

    against the river. They front-flip over the reeds,
past the rocks into the one spot deep enough

    to hold them. Then again. From the shade,

three girls are watching. You have to be brave,
    one says, to jump from the bridge. She means

the water is so cold it will swallow you.

    She means it's foolish to approach depths
you can never quite touch. The others look struck

    as Miranda first seeing mortal men. And they

are a spectacle, the boys, never even once
    glancing. True to just themselves. Thus unfolds

the pageantry of desire. You there. Me here.

    In the self-same space of wanting, cruelty is born.
Breaking from the rest, one boy ties the end

    of his t-shirt to form a net, thrusts it into

the water and emerges—almost too
        easy—with a fish. The others gather, and he hurls

the shirt against the concrete ramp. Again,

        again. Newly aware of his power, he makes sure
the girls observe this. He wants the other boys

        to see the girls see what his hands can do.

For the first time, the girls are terrified of men.
        O brave new world of the body. O beautiful

boys of America. Will you clap your friend

        on the back? Will you sidle next to the young
women and say something gentle?

Because there had to be one woman who first loved a man. Let's call
her X.

Because X started it.

Because I can't imagine her face.

Because I've been ghost-riding love since the beginning. Saying *go*, then
sitting outside of it.

Because choking ourselves in the elementary school bathroom until we
fainted got me hooked on the wrong kind of love.

Because X visits me at night. Rolls her eyes.

Because X never had a man's hand around her throat and was supposed
to like it.

Because the town I was born in opened its doors wide at night for some
mountain air. We woke up with deer in our kitchens, which
made me think no one could hurt me.

Because Stevie sang it: rulers make bad lovers.

Because I like watching others do unto each other what I don't want to do.

Because X was most likely beautiful. Because that somehow matters.

Because it's easy to give oneself up for beauty. But what about
  cockroaches. Would men have become saints for those.

Because, on a promised ride home, the car stalled outside of town while
  three men collapsed on top of me, the smallest one speaking for
  the first time that night: *I could love you.*

Because it's a lonely place, always-leaving.

Because *agape* was different than *eros,* and the soul has always been pushed
  above the body, and X must have believed in ideal forms.

Because, like all women of myth, X is my mother.

Because I would never die for love unless it was somebody else's. Like it
  was that easy, to wrap the body up so neatly. To say it, *Here
  I am, yours.*

{American Diptych}

I. Great Continental Divide

"We look," he announced—atop
the mountain valley vista point—

"like Adam and Eve." By which he must
have meant: pilgrims of desire. Form before

disaster. Their bodies looking mythic (Cranach's
golden hair) in a light that won't hold them

even close to forever. History crawling underneath
her ribcage and latching on. It takes, she thinks,

great arrogance to love where, one state earlier,
in Nevada, man ate another man and gold-hungry

settlers waited for letters that would never
come. All of which stems from:

they could have created all of this. In Wyoming,
one stream straddles the divide. One part runs east, one

west. This the hydrology she does not tell him,
their truck rewriting the settlers' trails

in the wrong direction. Unsettling. Split
across the body of the earth. Unbreakable wishbone.

Prolific rib. It becomes, from the Bering Strait
to the Strait of Magellan, an image they drive across.

See how one slides the humans like a cake topper.
See what distance affords, enlisting them.

This is a long division. In time, she hopes,
she will forget him. Not like the stream forgets

the water it grips so briefly—it remembers,
resembles nothing—but like no thing, no one.

II. Transcontinental Telephone Line

When the last wire was spliced, one hundred years
earlier in Wendover—where, after a day of driving,

we straddled the border of Utah and Nevada,
took pictures with our phones to send our loved ones

notice of safe passage—the East and West
could finally hear, together, a record's worn groove.

In 1914 one in Manhattan could transmit her longing
for one in Las Vegas in exactly the right tone.

On the phone, one didn't need a stranger dictating
the telegraph's missives, didn't labor with pen

over the best word, the most comely loop in the letter
L. Maybe, you said later, driving farther east toward your

new home, people said what they really meant
for the first time. Eleven days after the line was finally

finished, Franz and Sophie were shot in Serbia
and the world was dark for four more years.

"It appeals to the imagination to speak across
the continent," Woodrow Wilson told San Francisco

from the White House. *Wish you were here—*
So that, returning to California alone,

I can ask you, from our newly separate cities,
is it light where you are yet?

The Eye of God

> Because it is eternity, it embraces the whole of time, the past as well as the future. . . . In many respects, the drone dreams of achieving through technology a miniature equivalence to that fictional eye of God.
>
> —Grégoire Chamayou, *A Theory of the Drone*

Like, I want to say. For nothing's
                    new—think how the iron balls once soared

          above Gansu, 1227, bronze muzzle smoking
                              and impassive.

Consider the goose feather
          fletching it replaced, slipping the curved bow, below which

                              history keeps careening.
                    Imagine in tandem

the third-string QB's cannon
                    opening over Ohio

                    as Hannibal wakes
                              on the banks of the Agri.

          In league,
          the Pacific Fleet sinking

while Gainsborough empties again
and again those lonely skies in London. In Latin,

"war" can be confused,
in some forms, with "beautiful."

Jus in bello. That not beauty
must be just but

cavalry stampeding a chariot. The general booming Verdi
while Atlanta burns.

What of alien, infrared goggles
peeling back the night?

Silent engines that sit atop the clouds,
a narrator's governing ken? We fall so hard

for omniscience, allow—in a damp palm, or slid
under the teller's glass, *In God*

We Trust—one
prismatic eye to eye

us forever from its jade pyramid,
to stamp, always, its *yes*

of progress. All at once—
finger pressed to the encyclopedia's tense

spine, click after click—figurative, linked
                              up. Aramco burning.

        The spiking futures. *We are eyes*
                        on a vehicle flashing lights and it looks like

about 7 personnel to the east of that vehicle; how copy?
                        We are eyes

                              on Wrigley, overgrown with ivy.
                On Giotto's putti swimming alone

                in the dark.
Those great, flightless auks.

                              Assos' five Doric columns tilting faster
                toward the Aegean—*I, I, I, I, I.*

        Like
                        Was blind, but now I see—

King of Hearts

Inside his ice cream factory my father would lift me onto a counter
to watch him alchemize salt and cream until it hardened, to sift and bend
and taste, and he said *Open up* as he placed a whole vanilla bean
in my mouth. I didn't know what to do with it.
I don't know many things, like when to call a moon *Hunters'*,
but I do know when it gets too large to breathe I need to go
back inside and study iconography. I studied my father like a god
I didn't believe in. His ashy hair. His eyes like mud.
Kristeva said color is a shattering of unity—my father was a slow kind
of shattering. Men have often chosen me to be the woman
they cry in front of. A museum they can walk into. I've held
strangers' heads in my lap at parties. Turned confessional I was
suddenly wooden and capacious. I was holier than I had ever
been. When a man puts his hand in my mouth, I hope
I can make him cry for me. When the cat drags the rabbit
inside, I can't help listening for a heartbeat.
Jealous of a god so adored, I took a photograph of every
St. Sebastian in Europe. Arrow through the chest. *King of Hearts*,
my father's business. Like men could be bet on, or ruled.

Kiss Cam

Even I, pure in my loneliness, in line
                for the good soft pretzels, sprint back
      to my seat. Sentinel
for the bare-shouldered, the cutoff-clad and sugar-
         smudged, for tall boys trampled
              and the greased-up mustard pumps,
for men threshing against
              a particularly elusive curveball (brutal,
      the Bay's sure fog). For seabirds
diving the dumpsters, the chanted
        snatches of old cheers.
              The burnished, Pre-Raphaelite glow.
It trawls the crowd, patrons
           cast for tonight's brief drama.
        Here is the reluctant husband,
holding out until the final second
        for an automatic peck. The façade
           of searching, blur of faces, fireworks
bursting up, then the graying couple
          really going at it, tongue and all.
        Applause almost crushing the crowd
back into itself. Finally—each eager couple
        leans forward—the young parents
           score the finale. So intent
on righting a bag of popcorn

they nearly miss it, blush
at the audience's cheering and pull each other
close. They will, I think, remember this
always, a moment sponsored
by insurance ads and California
citrus, their faces hung between
zeros. At Gate 4 their photo
will be waiting. Real
as the syrup coursing through
the soda fountains, the snow cones
melting abstractly from their vivid
rainbows. They think they're not being transformed.
By time and its obstruction. By the lyric
strands of light framing their embrace.
Who doesn't want to be caught
like that? Trophy-bronze by the seventh,
twenty-nine forever, held
in the floodlights' blaze. Admit it—
beer flattening, sack of peanuts nearly
picked clean of duds—you want,
too, to be propelled
into pixel and hung
next to the late-summer moon.
You want to be the woman
bursting onto the screen alone
while the stadium around her burns.

On a Morning When Our Weather is 60 Degrees Different

it's like a stranger is standing between us.
        In California the drought has broken and, where you are,

first snow. It is the future, suddenly,
        to a past that was, to us, once kind. I imagine the stranger

looking down from a satellite, the line he could draw
        connecting us, bright dots on a distant map

on a planet that, out there, held at a certain length, still
        impresses. I mean all those first words from

the moon. I mean when we first found the written word
        and could alter what we had said. I said *No one is you*

but popular science tells me that, in other dimensions,
        that isn't quite true. On paper, I'll get it right

someday. "It's difficult," wrote Catullus, "to break
        with long love suddenly. But this you must somehow do."

Still, I try to like you best removed. Above all this,
        perspective like that of an interested god, would the weather

satellite turn the winter storm to peaceful swirl
        sent to your television set. Across the screen,

would the world slow a little. "O Gods, if you
        can pity or have ever brought help at last to any

on the point of death . . ." Sweet Catullus. To liken love
        and death. Our great mistake. When we saw our language

carved in stone, we fell in love with it a little
        and hoped ourselves, too, permanent things.

Love Letter to the President

> The Senate has quietly stripped a provision from an intelligence bill that would have required President Obama to make public each year the number of people killed or injured in targeted killing operations in Pakistan and other countries where the United States uses lethal force.
>
> —*The New York Times,* April 28, 2014

Dear sir:

In youth I collected names of the boys I did what with in a list numbered down sheaths of ripped out notebook paper. That same year I had to memorize the names and dates of all the presidents of the United States. The computer found each headshot so I could picture them alive and arrange their facts into a straight line. This was before you. This was when I skipped class to protest the new war, already astonished by what information I would never know. For four years in elementary school I delivered a basic report on the humpback whale. I knew the numbers by heart: 39-52 ft, 79,000 lb, 16,000 mi. I knew the taxonomy, for how else can a girl picture a monster men once thought was wingèd in foreign waters she will never touch? Within their own geography, the humpbacks will sing, continuously, for more than what we call a day. In these hours Atlantic whales will sound differently than those of the Pacific. Elvis, Buddy, Otis were the names of the first men I ever loved. I'd call up the local radio, request a familiar song and, knowing a voice sprung from death, thrill as the lyrics jolted a human something in a body that I've spent most my life trying to feel. I've heard you're trying to keep your data close. One needs the marginalia, but you're headline, sans serif, all-caps. Come back to me, please, a little smaller. In Paris, on a spring evening, Sartre to Beauvoir: "I wanted to bring you my conqueror's joy and lay it at your feet, as they did in the Age of the Sun King." I wanted to bring you this—one whale divided by water from another. One song changed throughout time, never repeating. I wanted to lay at your feet the boys I kissed in the dark and press their Austins, Jesses, and Bradys to your ear. To give you the clean detail of history. This age, sir, could be named for you.

Bad Intelligence

Pixelated, on a clear day, a shovel may resemble
a rifle. A woman is always a civilian, by definition,

and data. And data (416-957 civilians
in Pakistan) will not be updated. The ability

to loiter for longer along the largely erased
border will further, we are certain,

American interests. We named a drone Hermes,
after *Herma*, Greek for: prop, heap of stones, boundary

marker. O mighty messenger of the gods (—Aeschylus),
bringer of good luck, guide and guardian (—Homer),

thief at the gates, watcher by night (—anon.),
give us the full leaked report without seeking

permission for entry. Hermes, you who protect
trade and travelers. God of transition, and poets.

In Which I Misread the Title as *Devotional Paleontology*

Not the proper *Devonian*, age of fish.
     Because that's something I could kneel down for—
primitive sharks, continents of forests
        beginning their root systems, no thoughts of God.

"Time to Get Clean" says the Laundromat's sign.
     I could get clean for trilobites, mimic
their death curl, that sober relic. To devote myself
        hopelessly, to become a bucolic sea-field,

get all spiritual and undone underneath
     the fern explosion—that's better than any sleeping pill
I've mouthed. I could be lazy, in love
        with lycophytes. I could commit to conodonts, pray

to placoderms. Adopting their armor, couldn't I
     abandon the ocean, grow legs and walk
into the arms of a beautiful irreversible extinction?
        There was never a horizon two people

saw the same, but I have hope for the plants.
     Mouthless, ferns might adore my paranoia, stay
awake with me, cradling a bottle of wine.
     When the tide draws back to reveal its skeletons—

I've never understood where the water really goes.
  There's hope in the study of things.
That a lost world might stay a little longer. That amid
  all the myths of departure I could unhinge

my jaw, become the hagfish, co-opt
  that monster. And just be there, slime-slicked, tracing
my belly against the bottom of the earth.
  Of the ocean floor, I know nothing. That's nice.

Taking Down the Bridge

Treasure Island is on fire. Or
    so it seems, torches smoking
through the cantilever truss,
    hiding even the men
who wield them.
    When it is finished, next year,
perhaps, carefully dismantled
    in roughly the reverse of its creation,
58,000 tons of steel will be released
    and the new bridge—
gleaming white of the future—
    will stand alone. But now,
almost dusk, the old bridge is cut
    in two, as if the center, in fact,
could not hold, had fallen into
    the Bay with its weekday
sailboats. At Zeitgeist,
    yesterday, we drank beer
outside and listened to the youth
    of San Francisco get everything
wrong. You told me
    how you would bring old relics
into the classroom—an antique
    shoehorn, ophthalmologist's lancet,
a wine key made of bone—

and tell your students to become
archaeologists, to discover the objects
for the first time, create
a use for them, a name, saying
this is what poetry does.
"How wrong that now seems,"
you said. "Why must we make
everything new?"
Hegel understood this, I guess,
the demolition of the concrete
as necessary for progress.
That Being and Nothing unite
as Becoming. But the earrings
that will one day be made from
the bridge's picked-apart skeleton—
the eager group
at the bench next to us
will wear them beautifully.
And they will reflect
nothing, in their conserved rust.
Imagine, I wanted to tell you,
what of us, a century from now,
they will haul in to hold—
your ancient, hulking cell phone
that could be a paper weight,
a time machine,
a device for measuring love.

Anti-Blazon

My mister's eyes—my lovething, my

　　　　　　　　　guy—are not

　　　California's golden light. Not the Pacific

flickering its white caps to a plummeting

　　　plane. I find nothing

　　　　　　　　in his smile

that suggests his teeth are looted

　　　　　　　marble, no pillared Parthenon

　　　　　　　frieze. No victory

　　　garden grows upon his face.

When he speaks, nothing moony

　　　　　　　quickens its orbit. What,

　　you wanted me to sip

　　　　　　from his hip bones' goblets? *As*

　　if, poetry says. True—beauty

　　　　　　feeds on further, farther.

Like power. How

　　　from his desk the president

　　　　　　watches one

Hellfire then another *plucking*,

　　　　　he calls it, the familiar figuration

　　　　　　　of terror. Must we

　　fall so in love

　　　　　　with abstraction? Place our men

at arm's length? It takes miles,

                    making bearable a body
        that sweat-stains my sheets.
                    His goodly eyes not godly. His farewell
no crushing stone. I know,
                    our love is no real tragedy,
        is not precision
                    strike, not humming
drone. No, the dropping missile doesn't
        sing, muse.

At a Planned Parenthood Rally, a Man Tells His Son I Want to Kill Him

This is some kind of love—alien,
emerging from the Best Buy.
How he steers his son
right up to me, makes him look
at my face. As if to say, this
is the world—blond, soft—this is danger.
A freeway over, my father has only begun
to die. Already I've been with him
all my life in hospitals, been so bored
I wanted to get it over with. I've pushed him
to the asphalt, on a summer evening,
to complete a layup. I've fished
him out of the river with an oar
when his body was too weak to swim.
The boy is looking at me like I *would*.
Like I'd shove him in front of the next
speeding car, like people do
in movies. I wish I could give him
such drama. For a year in Texas I lived
with a man who my father, if he'd survived
the hospitals, would have, really, killed.
I want to believe in the father who
would turn a man over in his hands
and remake the world that would begin

unmaking me, the way it started
to unmake that boy, staring at me
with my sign, me smiling at him,
telling him I would never
hurt him, both of us knowing
that somehow wasn't true.

Deus Ex Machina (I)

Drama's most realistic
                here—we make it up
     as we go. I love you
I loved you I love
             Love, though he
   has wings.
And, as Shelley
        taught us,
   like light can flee.

So we banish sunset
      from the script. The couple
        never went to bed
still cross. They kept on
        sitting at the table, waiting
    forever for the moon.

Any woman
     can become hooked
        by a stagehand's artificial
wings. Failed
     plot point. Exit
forced. Like a finger
       they lift the machine.

The vatic feelers
                    shut off for love.
          Our hero, insofar
as she is human,
                    could not transcend
          the impatient final scene.

She improvises as desire
          does—turns blind
to the dénouement.
                    Reconciliation. Triumph
          over reason.
And the spectators
                    are satisfied.

The President Took No Questions

after another unarmed black boy was shot after
five speeches the war in Iraq isn't going badly five
years after the election Bush smiled at the cadets for years
it seemed a man like that could say anything doesn't it
repeat itself silence took no questions reporters repeat
will you accept censure from Congress to Bill
to Barack to Dick California quaked enough to
break open wine country's reserve barrels to break
news the day of Brown's funeral I watched new
faces on TV on silent from the elliptical which faces
west in a town where Condoleezza teaches west
of everything else I realize is one way everyone of
everywhere can describe a place when everywhere
hurts in that pathetic fallacy when pressing pause hurts
heads to really feel for Foley in orange allegedly beheaded
because of air strikes in Iraq which we're back in because

{Pennsylvania Triptych}

I. Elegy for the Sext

> But please, don't ask me who I am. A passionate, and fragmentary girl, maybe?
> —Sylvia Plath

It is true that, after a night of no communication, the Philae lander sent back the first image from a comet, which showed only one of its three legs touching down on the cracked surface.

After the lunar Salt Flats, after the brilliant soy fields of Iowa and the manic Pittsburgh truckers, we placed him in his new home. We photographed the columned monuments and admired how sharply the white marble still shone.

I imagine the pixel as a tactile thing. A being capable of touching another, in passing, for even the shortest period of time.

In Berlin, when the wall finally fell, citizens rented hammers to chip away souvenirs. *Mauerspechte*, they were called. Wall woodpeckers.

To participate in the demolition is to be a part of history. Is what I tell myself, flying back to California alone.

Him in the dim stall of a Gettysburg dive bar. Me in front of the mirror, in his phone, with my hand down my pants. Our parts-of-bodies crossing the nation.

Simone de Beauvoir knew, in the afterlife, she would never be joined with Sartre.

It is true that, once the body becomes fixed, it is too much itself.

It is possible, now, for anyone to own a piece of the wall. One can receive a graffitied, concrete block with the preordered purchase of a video game.

In the dark, while the game is loading, a screen reflects back one's face.

The spacecraft was named for the Philae obelisk, used to decipher Egyptian hieroglyphics.

Once the body becomes a downloadable thing, is it true?

I wake to a picture proving that if one rises early enough, in Pennsylvania, one might see an employee wiping Hancock's bronze cheek.

That the part represents the whole, in this space, after a night of no communication.

Hoe, mouth, man with hand in mouth: Egyptian hieroglyph for love.

II. Cyclorama

> In this way you look out on the perfectly painted sky . . .
> with nothing whatever between you & the landscape.
>   —General John Gibbon, Union Army 2nd Corps

Outside the Visitor Center—patrons queuing up in
khaki camo shorts, baseball caps, *Where Big Bucks
Lie*, boxes of MoonPies wheeling by—two men
with rubber gloves, with Windex, on a July
Monday, polish the bronze Lincoln. His massive
hands. A crown of flies. The mothers kneel before
braided girls and deliver unto them their palms of
glistening sun block. Five boys are pinned with
badges, are aiming their bottles of pop like rifles, at
Laura, quick to dive behind some benevolent skirt.
The fathers. Biceps white and Semper Fi-ed.
Faithful, always, to the easy turning away, the How
about those. . . . Finally, glass doors shirring wide, a
stream of air, cool as metal, admits the line inside.

Step inside the center. Leave behind the liter-Cokes, boiled hotdogs, the Skittles melting to a child's palm. Leave behind the texts, the seventh grade history. See with what valor the men in gray rise toward Pickett's Charge to be picked from earth like ants. The argument is to remove simile from the picture. To let realism reign. Look closer—the most exact feature is made from abstract streaks. Blocks of color, blurred brushstrokes. So faithful, from afar, veterans claimed it was they who slumped against the oak's good weight. *We laid you / upon your long bed, and our officers / wept hot tears like rain and cropped their hair.* The bayonets and buckles held a certain gleam—tinsel. Workers hauled sod by the cartload, fixed the foreground with relics. Fences, canteens. A shoe. None were embalmed with honey. Their horses bloated under heavy rain.

ooooo

You see the horses first. One just fallen, on the dirt path toward Vicksburg, dappled gray. His soldier crushed. A rebel cuts another from the carriage's ropes. Foreground: blood along a tawny neck. One—white, majestic— bucks his rider, is always bucking his rider, forever, from history. Might it be easy to look away from the surgeon's bone saw. From the man slung between two others like a sack of flour. The barn wall left gaping, red brick exposed around the edges. Like flesh. The stone wall singed black. Meade holds and holds, but barely. Cannons bruise the air, the open field (Lt. Col. Franklin Sawyer, 8th Ohio) moans. *The grey wave crying / unearthly lamentation over the water* of the wheat, the rippling smoke. Never can the low stone become crossable. Never can the blond youth slump back atop his steed, the saber un-stick itself from the rib-gap, nor the flesh above the knee. It's hard not to admire the trees—dwarfing our toy drama. They rise in plumes, toward . . . some thing. Three hundred seventy seven feet of canvas tacked around the room.

When Boston tired of viewing the battle, it took an entire day just to roll up the canvas. Poor panorama. Poor painted soldiers molding in a vacant lot, history too large to store, all six tons. Poor

Paul Philippoteaux who chose *this* moment to paint (tattered gray, death march across the farm's slow fences) as if it could have been otherwise. As if the South hadn't only overshot (visibility poor

for smoke, bullets sailing over the high blue caps) here. How art makes its masterpiece regardless, its illusion. In the round room, a narrator seals us inside our fate. The lights dim. The smoke pours

through the landscape beautifully (rosy-fingered, almost)—we hear the cannons first. Then dawn speeds up. We're flung straight through to lyric. We, astonished readers of history, lean forward. But

the thick railing holds us back. Denies the moment. We are some shameless wheel, churning clockwise around the room. Once we spoke respectfully, in the lobby, of grandchildren, two-for-one

specials, cold beer. It was before these men were born. Before the cotton boll split its firm seed for canvas. Before the pines were tapped for turpentine. We ascended the escalator's soundless por-

tal, once, didn't we? Weren't we gaping at the wall of ammunition glass-sealed below? Weren't we working the restroom's hand dryers, queuing up for the show, tiring already of our astonishment?

Georgia vets loved the show
the immutable charge where
they saw a new war a new
way to fix the past as if it
weren't always lapping back
into chaos *In the beginning how
the Heavens and Earth / Rose
out of Chaos* how the ads sold
it Glorious Gettysburg in all
the Awful Splendor of Real
War Napoleon desired one
for each of his battles *his*
battles he called them but
what does art know of chaos

ooooo

"I know! It's all so sad... I never could have
done it, march across, like, a wide-open field.
How many stadium lengths did he say? That
sounds right. No, *that* one's Little Round Top.
Where we ate our lunch. What? Well, *she* can
hush! This isn't church. These men weren't
gods. I mean, they probably all owned slaves—
we shouldn't feel that bad. They chose their
side, to fight. There wasn't some *draft*. I'm sick
of reading about their valor. Yeah, I heard they
survived on horsemeat. Like, married their
younger cousins. I would have shot the
prisoners instead. Why even paint it, as if
they're good? That isn't *my* past."

ᴑᴑᴑᴑᴑ

So, if only in art, our past is good,
wrapped around us like a flag, if it
is something from which we have
all emerged, gods of no lasting evil,
no certain slur remaining across a
Baptist church, no hung epithet
from a state house, nothing sung
from the pink-faced Sigma Alpha
Epsilons in Norman, OK, en route
to the Azalea Ball, their belles
hoop-skirted & waiting to rise, still,
from the South, (*You can hang 'em
from a tree / There will never be a* ___
SAE) we are most forgetful gods.

Say the CSA *wasn't* all in rags Say they
would have been in pretty good shape,
in gray Say a *Gone With the Wind* post-
war cliché may have gotten the best of us
(Say you didn't swoon, one adolescent
winter day, for Rhett) Say the derby is
better with a wide brim, a julep refreshed
from a silver tray Say states' rights Say
bellum Say it's best to show the enemy a
little frayed Say a word more lovely than
magnolia Say *we, for our part, will blot out
the memory / of sons and brothers slain* Say
Aunt Jemima's happy likeness proves the
plantation was okay Say it straight-faced

Facing it, the cylindrical room that holds us close
to the past, you might forgive a little. As if, ante-
bellum, white and wealthy, with your father's
father's sprawling fields, you wouldn't have let the
house staff serve you pheasant. The sold-out
showings prove this—in Atlanta and Pyongyang,
in the Kunstmuseum Thun and Berlin, Ohio—
how we have in us a taste for beauty and for
terror. Nowhere in these scenes—"prisons of
paint," one patron remarked—is a young mother
bending to slip a child's foot into a sandal. No
expanse of poppied hills. Vicksburg, Waterloo.
We want to think we are a benevolent kind. That
we split the canvas, stepped through all that past.

"Not at all! That way's south. It *is* disorienting at first. Yes, this is my twenty-ninth visit, so I guess you could say I am. Of course— you can't beat Garryowen. I have dreams about their fish n' chips. Have you been here for Bike Week? Man, it's wild. Thousands of Harleys, the whole town growls. And on the 4th, you'll see three Robert E. Lees sipping Bud Lights at the same bar! Chamberlain peeling out of the McDonald's parking lot. No, my wife would never let me camp out with all those kooks. I only get one night. Why the Civil War? My great great uncle fought. Tennessee. I found it out on ancestry.com. Oh, sure, let's see… if you look closely, that soldier there, he's painted with Lincoln's face. Shot dead, dragged—they won't tell you that. Why aren't any of the soldiers black? I guess I never noticed. Don't mention it! Right, just head straight down Carlisle. And tell them Big Gabe sent you!"

Augusts the co-eds march Carlisle for orientation. Their folks have taken the weekend for an educational vacation, get drunk in hotel bars. The fathers debate statistics from their four-hour car-tours ("Lee lost 13,500 at Chancellorsville, not here!") where the sons practiced affect and yawned. Gathered on the cemetery's lawn, the freshmen snap photos of the un-marked graves. In one, a young woman waves an Eagles scarf. Another frames a group of guys mimicking war. Such ease with the past. Who wouldn't trade marble fact for one last night in a dimming dorm?

The problem might be that art outlasts us. That it casts us for a future eye. That it unmasks us before a people we never knew. The problem might be formal. A circle proposes a point at which it is complete. Where you can meet your spouse at the egress, step out into a cooling Pennsylvania night. The problem could merely be some small desire to stand a little longer inside the comfort of the room. Too, it could be that, afterward, in bed, it is not the musket-shot, not the blood-soaked scene, the reason these men fought that survives in your small talk, but the way the artist so smartly painted himself among it all, leaning against that tree.

"I don't see how you can be against it, those men all fought for a way of life you never knew. Sure, those guys in blue get heaps of praise, but— what's that quote about books, and victors? You know what I mean. That's easy for *you* to say. What if some government thug showed up tomorrow and took your nice job away? I mean, there's *truth* to that. You think Reconstruction was all fun and games? Did every three-year-old granddaughter in a white bassinet deserve your blame? No, hey. Slow down. I'm not saying slavery was okay, you're putting words in my mouth. I'm just saying that the South did suffer. And I'm not sure any veteran of our country should be treated like that. Not American? Please. Brothers fought brothers, and you're saying one shouldn't claim a country? That their mothers didn't have a right to weep? That we should just sweep away the fact that Yankees bought up that cotton, that *their* machines were run by kids? Lady I'm not some ignorant hick."

ooooo

Sometimes, it's enough to make you love
your country. The girl's face lifted to the
cyclorama's drape of sky. The boy afraid
of the cannon's noise. The parents
fumbling through a crude guide—they
could have gone to Disney World.
Cancun. But here, they have left their
backpacks, mandatory, at the visitor's
desk. They obey the lines, hush properly
when the narrator's recorded voice
unfurls the soldiers' fates. They will drive
back, late, to Annapolis, to Jersey, the
long mini-van haul to Cleveland, taking
some vision of the past for the future

III. Field Trip

What, though, could they learn
here, Pennsylvania's slate sky

dull above the cortege of worn out buses,
with brown bag lunches

and the sheer fact of sex
they haven't quite yet come

to acknowledge, though the boys
are trying to toss grapes

down a poor girl's blouse,
are pelting her now with their

intent, and just as quickly
as it begins, this game

of the body, the boys lose interest
when some gust blows a bag

of chips—flashing like tinsel
between the boulders—

out of their sweaty hands
and they're shrieking

down Little Round Top,
receiving the good girls' glares,

girls who have witnessed
their mothers' stern admonishments

and know this is a kind
of love, where they come from,

a town whose history
holds less blood

than the ground they've walked
all morning, dutifully

behind their teachers, and they're sick
of it now, the suffering

of men with such foreign names—
Ambrose, Gustav—men

who even in their towering bronze
likenesses are no match

for Tommy (the boys cry)
who is thrusting his hips at the base

of a cannon, so obvious, see,
it is almost painful, the extravagance

of his whooping, the others
in line to mimic this mythic

motion, and they are facing
the field, wreathed in light

and granite markers where men—
barely older than those here

today—lay down, expired,
but that is too much

for this group to imagine,
they who do not yet know

they will die, they whose
febrile energy is narrowed

to Laura's sloping nape,
the soft hair, there, perfect

for the wad of gum
being placed, tenderly,

tenderly, into the divot
below her ear, below her nimbus

of curls, this is how brief
their memory,

for they have just been lectured
on Jennie Wade—the small town's sole

civilian casualty, July 3rd, the South
already dissolving—

"Gin" her mother called her,
who was kneading biscuits

meant for the surrounding Union
troops when a bullet

passed through one door
of her small house, then another,

her back, her heart,
which is still beating, if you are to believe

the ghost tours leading
visitors through humid summer nights

these students will not
feel, they will be back in their own

air-conditioned rooms—how just,
youth—and if the soldiers exist

at all for them then, it will be
in their names, German, remnants

of an older world lapping at the back
of their sleeping throats, which will be sore

after so much laughter, so much
instinctual laughter they will leave behind.

FaceTime

> It's like a modern Aladdin's lamp—you rub it, in this case it's a
> camera. You push a button and it gives you the things you want.
>   —Weegee

What I wanted was

    another way to spin the story.
To be the shop window dummy
    Weegee fell in love with,

numbed, naked—not

    for you. To be the breaking
news, as, 2,000 miles
    removed, your face shows up

inside my phone.

    I turn my tabloid day
around the room,
    try to arrange each accident—

to lick the blade, spilled bag

    of lentils, the date gone
wrong—into image
    enough. I'm supposed

to make you feel

      like you were there
all along. Weegee wanted to look
      at the lookers, to turn

their lives to smut.

      What I did was
simply this, Weegee stated. *I went down*
      to Manhattan Police Headquarters

and for two years I worked

      without a police card
or any kind of credentials.
      And naturally, he said,

I picked a story that meant

      something. I pick an angle
that doesn't mean
      I've been waiting. Lighting

to show how bare

my face. I know, now,
why Weegee loved the nudes—
        where light reaches,

turns the body grotesque.

        Even a drunk must be
a masterpiece. I'm a piece
        of work, you tell me,

when I ask how is it

        with your other girls. What
I wanted was to see
        you leave me, to watch

the drama unfold.

        Instead, you reach
the phone outside
        your top floor apartment

and dangle me, face-down,

        above the street.
See, you say, how small
        the people look from here?

A Habitable Space

scientists have it better
at the end of the day they

can actually *touch* something

where the word exhale means
nothing nor boundary

acreage asylum how can

one have sympathy for
an exoplanet where no one will

bend toward a neighbor's garden

to pick a lime from the tree
where legend does *not* have it

I'm tired of all the not-saying

what is seen is not what is felt
or the drone would never

Post-

winter, the ice caps mostly unlocked,
postlapsarian, post-VHS, post-Pac, it will be harder
to evince sympathy from the gods. Post-Prince.
The world formerly known as woolly mammoths
fumbling toward some heat. Post-puberty
I fumbled in the dark cars of skinny boys
and popped Natty Light tops, crop top
pulled off. Post-pill paradise. Post-9/11, I called
the cops on a junior tossing stink bombs
outside Señora Compton's class (she bolted
the door as we dove under our desks). I shared
post-shift joints with our manager, Marissa,
Burger King walk-in filling with smoke. Post-
mortem, my father looked like an ancient king
ruling from his living room cot. Post-God.
Post-Plato, poets really got a bad rap—
flaunting our heroes' breakups and breakdowns,
making even Odysseus weep like a girl. No more
lamentations of famous men. No more
steamy Olympus shower scenes. Poster child
of the post-game hand job, arcade backroom
queen, I paid for the Twizzlers my boyfriend lifted
from their giant plastic tubs. Post-
grunge. Post-graduate, pouring wine
for post-Yuppie Portland accountants,

I practiced my affect. I practiced Post-it note
GRE prep on my Honda's dashboard
before my shift. Before I left the city,
post-certainty, post-cash, I posted pictures
of my couch, my bookshelves, my ratty mattress
that a stranger carried down three flights
of stairs. I learned a postmodern side-eye,
how to get by post-truth. I learned
that the word disaster means bad star,
that the planets might be positioned
poorly but good god when we're close enough
Mars burns red hot in a corner of the western sky.

On the Theory of Descent

—Darwin

He meant, of course, origin. What
                    strains from what framework
                                of bones. The form

                        the giraffe bends
                down to the dirt same as the elephant,
                    binding our foreign, numbered

weight. And from the war
        of nature comes the production
                    of a higher animal. Say

                                    from the war of nature comes
                        what we need—
            a machine more than man. What mind wouldn't

want this? Clean tactic, poor boys
            of America safe before a screen.
        My friend—caught, in Jalula

                        by an IED—not quite right
                still. Who am I, then, to demand
                        a higher order.

There is grandeur,
Darwin says, in this view of life.
The new technology

that keeps our Global Hawk air-strong
thirty-four long hours. Improving the real
bird's endurance by a day. So art

plays nature's second part.
Coiled, darker
than black, the engine resembles

sci-fi's most gleaming
machinations. Death-helmet, snake
pit, asteroid-flung. Endless forms

most beautiful. It looks ready
for space,
some thicker atmosphere.

Over Gaza
men call drones *zanana*—nagging
wife. Slang imitating sound. How hungry

language becomes. *Thy soul was like*
a star—They are as gentle as zephyrs,
blowing below the violet—

Her beauty hangs

           upon the cheek of night—Always

we want more. Catch up, fiction. We are

already our most gruesome

        design. Operators, in their padded

    chairs, in low, tan Midwestern

                buildings, cannot hear

              the buzzing—*like*

      a thousand chainsaws—these new birds

make. *Bangana*—Pashtu for wasp—

    sing us a song we can fall down

        into. Sing something decent, something

     far off and sweet. We are, we now know,

        made from star stuff. Who *wouldn't* feel

           god-like, so hovering, so composed.

A Bad Date

The pleasure boats cut across the lake we can see
    from the hotel restaurant's floor to ceiling windows.
"I'm a sucker for a view," I say, which, he tells me,
    dignifies imperialism. What with Rome, and all.
We're meeting to see if I will let him, tonight,
    tie me to not-his-bed, to, with the instruments
he will deem necessary, knock against me while
    his wife watches. I'm trying to forget another
man, so I repeat what I have heard on the radio:
    to assuage traffic jams, engineers are studying
ants. Sans egos, they get where they need to go.
    No flash. No honking. No aggressive driving.
Outside is only an inch of glass away. I sip my wine.
    The fog bank has been erasing the hills
for a week, and in the mornings I climb the stairs
    to my apartment's balcony, where what is visible
is mine, and I would kill for it, the right-out-there.

Love Letter to _____, Unmanned Aircraft Systems
Operator

Dear you,

    When you go home at night,

        does your machine sleep

            too?

Is the freezer you walk to,

        three A.M.,

      a point on the screen,

   each cube of ice

      dropped into your glass

a little click?

    In that moment, falling

      through space—the ether

        in which alone

   the gods are gods—

there must be

      some rote pleasure in the clink.

       O operator,

      sight for the machine—

I doubt everything I see.

      I see how you could do it.

Elegy

My wrist is still marked   with the stamp of a black star   from a club
three nights ago.   He was him   because now he isn't.   Father because
not mother.   Missed   because not seen.   None of the doctors
had names—   my willful erasure.   Skin did not yellow   but gild.
When he called   me *bitch*   I made it song.   It was   because it wasn't
silence.   Dancing with a stranger   holds the trace   of first falling into
a father's arms.   And all those recent   unearthed bodies,   royalty
mummified by being   cherished and forgotten   are brought up
from the dirt   to prove   what?   How much we love men   when
they're   silent and permanent.   Listen—I'm still keeping him   alive.
Daughter because not   son, because afflicted.   The stamp is part of me
like he is, fading.   Original lack.   Body as theory.   Anthologized body
re-read.   I turned my father into ash   so he could never   be resurrected.

Simone Weil Walks Alongside Her Brother After Supper

After winter's thaw, the hollow-pit stomach
blunted with hunger, Phaedra's first words
char her ears—*Let's go no farther.* The wood-smoke
disgusts her. The physician, who kissed her hand
exiting, disgusts her. Too, the torn seam of her dress.
Forgotten lines, disgust her. And in her head she
goes *Bright god of fire* goes *O Sun.* No, no farther from
heat, grabs her brother's wrist. She knows night
is an equation of undoing. She does not sleep,
just feels over her body for gracelessness. Injury.
Kinks her fingers inside her self. Does not sleep,
lest the moment, waking, when the sky is still
missing. Has been inside her body too long.
No, farther from the house of diseases and dinners,
of open doors—*The world my life degrades.* André stops,
points to the bleach-white egg on the side of the road,
questions the intellect of its design. The way it is so
round. He is always pointing out flawed things,
such as men do (*By which his pure hand must not be profaned*).
This does not disgust her, yet. Just the way the world gets
under the skin and flourishes. She palms the egg,
vulgar thief. Vulgar girl. Later, incubating it
with her young and ungoverned love—*I had touched it*—
excited by its delicate potential for ruin,
yolk unseen—*It is a thing defiled and stained*—her
zealot, crushed, she finds it is not alive. Is loaded.

Love Letter to MQ-1C Gray Eagle

Drone, you have seen me pick a fig straight from the tree
and eat it whole, standing up. This is how lovers
consume things, in the moment, making the flies jealous.

We could get on like this, at a distance. When I trace
the one cloud that eats all other clouds, I could pretend
to see you. I could flash you my mediocre breasts.

Mostly, though, I want to know your thoughts on hard
science-fiction. Do you think of all the possibilities of living
in an astral belt? Do you get all twisted inside

thinking about getting off on Mars? Me? I think the *The X-Files*
got a bit too religious. About God *and* aliens. Besides,
I know my own capabilities. If I close my eyes hard enough,

I can see distant planets exploding. Or maybe they're being
birthed. Maybe you see this too, my wherever-you-are,
my keeper. Maybe you see me feed small, white moths

to my cat, then cry in the shower after. I'm often
sorry about what I do, even if I don't stop my actions.
I often want to suck my words back into my mouth.

Because of you, when my arms are upraised to the sky,
they are also appraised. Show me my worth, drone,
in the back alley, hidden from every eye but yours.

My metalcraft, my no-see-um, my I-dare-you-to-come-
down-from-there—if you require no hands and I require no
privacy, aren't we destined to be less human together in the dark?

The Quarry

Weekends we passed it on our way to bonfires and tapped kegs, changing,
backseat, from our sweat-soaked jerseys to something small that glittered.
Brad would back his Jeep to the turnoff's dusty edge and blast,
from his three 15"s, "Juicy" all night. We grasped our Solo cups.
I was always flat-backed against a large oak, Kaila peeing quietly
in the woods behind me while Trevor or Dustin or Will asked me to repeat,
again, my name. Which sounded, bass knocking hard all around us,
like *quarry*. Which I had to push again into their ears. Not pit of slate.
Not open mouth, not quartz-flecked men-worked ditch.
Ours wasn't the wide, sheer-cliffed pool we saw in movies. It wasn't
that glamorous. It held, we heard, the body of a sister or brother, a cousin,
surely, of a sophomore or senior from our school, from the next town
over, from a century earlier when our mothers' mothers walked, too,
its rim. We crushed our cans. We tossed them to the soil's craquelure.
It seemed, up there, some rushed facsimile of an ancient text telling *This
is how you breathe.* The stones we skipped across the gutted surface really stars,
the stars really planets of bright teeth. My girl-skin smelled of gypsum.
My name not origin of cut rock, not of boys driving too fast
down dirt roads with a hand resting between their knees. We inscribed
all their names. We walked, just drunk enough, through the fire.

The Age of Reason

The cover
of the *Times*—a café
window, shot
through, wine glasses
intact. The fashion
bloggers and concert
goers, the wine
connoisseurs, thought first
of the gun shots, dull
across the city
night, nothing.
Gang violence again,
that ordinary reflex
rehearsed. So we make
of suffering
a still life. This
is not human,
said the Pope
after. This is not
what we do. But.
The *we* who drink
the aperitif—spirit
to stimulate the appetite,
dry, not sweet—
lean forward. In 1943

Paris, German soldiers
applauded Cocteau, Sartre.
Camus flourished. Art
marched on. Sweet,
some said of life
in an occupied
country. Evening strolls
along the Champs-Élysées.
Piaf serenading
the brothels,
stuffing herself
on chocolate and pâté.
How silverware still
held its office
on the smartest of tables.
Yet the women who ate
from German
plates—Paris
paraded them naked
in the streets. Painted
swastikas across
their chests. Yes,
it feels good
to be right. We
are hungry for it,
the clumsy lesson.
In stadiums,

still, English soccer fans
slosh their beer,
spread their arms wide
for the Germans, imitating
the bombers
that left their country
a ruin to be proud of
and it is marvelous
to see so many men
nearly alight. They feed
from each other,
don't they, beauty,
disaster. After
the blasts, children
filed from the stadium.
Faces painted blue,
white, red. Sweet.
And across Niagara Falls
the lights shone
the French flag's colors
tumbling, alongside
us, down.

Predator

Which would make one think it had a hunger—

      glistening spit strung

from maw to marrow, polar bear ripping at its bearded seal.

      Nothing about the etymology

surprises. *Cervi luporum praeda*, as deer destined for

      wolves, dear Horace comparing

Carthage's doomed legions to beasts. Barbary lions pacing the Colosseum's

      bowels while, on high, the emperor's thumb

twitched. Buckling their knees, those last bladed elephants sighed.

      Who, then, the predator? Who, pray tell,

the prey? Victors, the Roman poet knew, lap too from the darkest

      of pools. Centuries, vast leagues

turning Rome to myth. Which is one way war becomes palatable—

      quite, of course, like rotting grapes.

Deus Ex Machina (II)

When the plot
        falters, from the crane
rises a god,
              Greek,
       to cement the script.
Behind the skene,
        crude rigging.
Pulley & hook &
           here is our hero
       descending
from an invisible sky.
       We're meant to believe
this—a world
          cut into, the worm
     in the apple's
taut core
      dug out
with the playwright's knife.
          See, reader,
     the near certain
hand. The effective
     tool. Above
the moon is cardboard
         & pockless—

          long prelude
to an inevitable
          end—& guides our hero
home—

Spolia

Like nations, love,
we grow from our own
vanquished pasts. Consider the way
I touched you, just now,
replica of ____ who took my hand
and showed how he
had learned he liked it. ____
who I told, minutes before my flight,
not to follow me. Another
wanted me to lie completely still
on top of him, covering his entire
body as he fell asleep. Sweet, now,
____ in memory. Sweet reuse.
The men who built the arch
after Constantine's triumph knew
to preserve older reliefs
of victory. Yes, the golden times
remembered, the past's good rulers still
in their chariots, but also the head
of an earlier emperor
replaced by Constantine's soft face.
May we, too, name old cities
after ourselves, become sole rulers
of a map corner, a coast.
When I say your name it will be

with the same language, the same mouth
used with all others. After death,
a triumphant emperor
was represented at his own funeral
by an actor. If he, the actor,
mourned, he did so in silence,
his stillness rehearsed.

Recessional

After the cake—
five-tiered, chocolate ganache, complete
with actual orchids
atop the fondant—the long buildup
to the last

last song, the father
of the bride slumped—one
too many courtyard cocktails—
in his chair, and after the pink
jasmine, andromeda, the dusty

garden roses softening
in a cut-glass vase in a corner
of the ballroom. After
pâtes de fruits, lemon tartlets.
After the toasts.

After the dinner served alfresco,
underneath tree boughs
and bistro lights. After the three-piece band
has exhausted
its covers,

the bride,
in her fitted-bodice blush
pink gown,
declares their exit. The fireworks write
their postscript across the sky

and not one of us thinks what we look like
from above, nor of
the eleven-vehicle wedding procession
delivering the newlyweds
to the groom's remote village.

A pilotless plane
pauses. One man looks up.
We know the rest from headlines.
How the attendants
leapt from their cars before

they caught fire.
Broken glass. Scraps of hot metal
striking the bride's face. Scorched
trucks and sandals left
scattered on the road. Seconds later

the echo beyond
the stone-built houses, the riverbed,
the highlands. Yes, one man,
the article says, looked up
when the familiar hum

of the drone—this
is what the sky now sounds like—
stopped. Imagine,
though, the moment before. The bride's hand
on her mother's wet cheek.

Keep the groom's son
breathing, the truck
intact. Poetry says, there is eternity
in the moment.
But as we with our sparklers

light the path for our
new couple to their limousine
door, as they raise the window
behind which they will become
invisible,

we see only ourselves. "Our art,"
                wrote Petrarch,
"is that which makes men immortal
                through fame." Turning back
to gather our summer shawls and high heels

        from the dance floor,
we recount, already, the day. The bride's smart
                braids. The ribbon
holding each cloth napkin. The balloons
                rising away

        from the city. What love poem
could be written when men can no longer
                look up?
In their thank you notes—
                calligraphed perfectly

in plum ink—the bride and groom include
                a candid photograph for each
attendee. In the moment,
        we didn't even know
                we were touching.

Love Letter to Who Owns the Heavens

cujus est solum ejus usque ad coelum
—13TH C. common law

Before man dreamed up the flying machine
                 we owned the air as far above our land

          as we could imagine. Up to infinity. Down
to hell. Because air, in the days of tangible

property, was nothing. No foot had emerged
               from a lander onto the foreign terrain

          of the moon. No satellites passing over the hostas.
The act of a horse, law says,

reaching his head into an adjoining field
               and biting another horse is a trespass.

          A word, freed from the lips, is in the air
a trespass. Now, in a country divvying up

the sky, unmanned machines will be given
               innocent passage. People will walk around

whispering *dominium* as if to control at least
their breath. So, before the space of utterance

is duly regulated, before the 83 feet of air
                    we own above our heads begins its collapse,

            this: I love you from the depth of the earth
to the height of the sky. I love you upon

land immovable, soil open to exploitation
                    by all. I am for your unreasonable use alone.

        And, when the wingèd gods finally interfere
with your possessor's enjoyment, to an

indefinite extent, I'll remember a time when
                    men were the ones doing harm with

            their own hands. I'll remember the words I once
had to give to you, on the porch, in private.

Acknowledgments

My gratitude to the editors of the journals in which the following poems first appeared:

The Adroit Journal: "On the Theory of Descent"
Beloit Poetry Journal: "The Eye of God"
Boston Review: "Bad Intelligence"
Colorado Review: "The Age of Reason"
The Cortland Review: "A Habitable Space"
Crazyhorse: "Post-"
Four Way Review: "A Bad Date"
Georgia Review: "The Quarry"
Handsome: "Elegy," "FaceTime," and "Simone Weil Walks Alongside Her Brother After Supper"
Indiana Review: "King of Hearts"
The Iowa Review: "Deus Ex Machina (I)," "Elegy for the Sext," "On a Morning When Our Weather is 60 Degrees Different" and "Spolia"
Kenyon Review: "Love Letter to Nike Alighting on a Warship" and "The President Took No Questions"

Linebreak: "Desiderata"

Meridian: "Love Letter to the President"

The Missouri Review: "Taking Down the Bridge"

Narrative: "Field Trip"

The New Yorker: "Kiss Cam"

Ninth Letter: "In the Year of No Sleep" and "Love Letter to Who Owns the Heavens"

The Normal School: "Love Letter to MQ-1C Gray Eagle"

Passages North: "In Which I Misread the Title as *Devotional Paleontology*"

Pleiades: "At a Planned Parenthood Rally, a Man Tells His Son I Want to Kill Him" and "Recessional"

Southern Indiana Review: "The Goodly Creatures of Shady Cove" and "Transcontinental Telephone Line"

West Branch: "Great Continental Divide" and "Love Letter to _____, Unmanned Aircraft Systems Operator"

Vinyl: "Apologia From the Valley of Inheritance" (as "Love: A Chronicle")

Virginia Quarterly Review: "Cyclorama"

"Recessional" was reprinted in *The Best American Poetry 2020*.

"Bad Intelligence" was reprinted in *Poems for Political Disaster* (Boston Review).

"The Age of Reason" was reprinted in *Poetry Daily*.

This book has been changed and changed again, just as I have been, by the company and wisdom of many different poets and communities.

First I must thank the Wallace Stegner Program at Stanford University for the time and support, for bringing me to the landscape so central to this book, and for the greatest gift of all—an embarrassment of brilliant writers and thinkers. Eavan Boland, Simone Di Piero, Ken Fields, Doug Powell—your workshops were essential, rooms in which one could almost feel the mind expand.

To those generous souls who have spent time with this book, all of my gratitude. Austin Allen, Kai Carlson-Wee, Brittany Cavallaro, Emily Rose Cole, Allison Davis, Hugh Martin, Matthew Miller, Rosalie Moffett, Sarah Rose Nordgren, Kelly Pieper, Jacques Rancourt, Michael Shewmaker, Emily Skaja, Casey Thayer, Brian Tierney—thank you, thank you.

For helping me deepen and further my thinking about the poetics of the drone, thank you to my AWP co-panelists Jill McDonough, Philip Metres, Solmaz Sharif, and Nomi Stone.

Much of this book wouldn't have been written without the assistance of a National Endowment for the Arts Literature Fellowship—thanks, especially, to Mo Sheriff. I'm also grateful for the continued support and community of the Bread Loaf Writers' Conference, and to Ellen Bryant Voigt, Keith Ekiss, and Bruce Snider for their insight up there on these poems.

"Cyclorama" wouldn't exist without John Drury—thank you, John, for your kindness and patience, and for your love of sonnets. Thank you, too, to Gregory Pardlo for the keen edits and thoughtful discourse as this sequence found its final form and home. Many thanks to Gettysburg College for the Emerging Writer Lectureship, which gave me a crucial new place to fall for and contend with, and to the National Parks Arts Foundation for the chance to participate as Artist in Residence at the Gettysburg National Military Park.

Thank you to those editors and judges whose kindness and faith in these poems has buoyed me for years—it's nearly impossible to say how much I appreciate your careful and lasting eyes and ears.

Many thanks to Paisley Rekdal for choosing "Recessional" for inclusion in *The Best American Poetry 2020*.

Endless gratitude to Amy Quan Barry, Kathy Fagan, and Linda Gregerson for spending time with this book, and for their wonderfully generous words of support.

It's been a great privilege to work with everyone at Tupelo Press, and I can't thank enough Kristina Marie Darling, Jeffrey Levine, David Rossitter, and Jacob Valenti for all their time and care seeing this manuscript through. Thank you, too, to Dede Cummings for her gorgeous work designing this book.

Finally, to Christopher Kempf, my first and best reader, who has been reading these poems for years, and without whom many of them wouldn't have been possible—I will be thanking you forever. It will never be enough.